The Fable of Mable with the Ladle at the Table

Written by Lavelle Carlson

Illustrated by Lucas Adams

A Phonemic Awareness Tale

The Fable of Mable With the Ladle at the Table
A Phonemic Awareness Tale

Written by Lavelle Carlson
Illustrated by Lucas Adams

Inquiries should be addressed to:
Children's Publishing
201 Woodland Park
Georgetown, Texas 78628

First Edition

ISBN: 0-9725803-1-X
Library of Congress Catalog Card Number: 2003095189

Carlson, Lavelle
The fable of Mable with the ladle at the table / written by Lavelle Carlson ; illustrated by Lucas Adams. - 1st ed. - Georgetown, Tex. : Children's Publishing, c2003.
27 p. : col. ill. ; 29 cm.
"A phonemic awareness tale"
Summary: To overcome their hesitation to try unfamiliar foods, Mable gives children such outrageous choices that they are willing to "settle for peas!" Entertain while teaching phonemic awareness, skills and sounds targeted, and word and syllable levels. Includes teacher information on phonemic awareness levels, skills and sounds targeted, and word and syllable levels.
ISBN: 0-9725803-1-X
1. Food - Juvenile fiction. 2. Food preferences - Juvenile fiction. 3. English language - Diction - Juvenile fiction. 4. Auditory perception. 5. Speech perception. 6. Reading (Primary). [[1. Food. 2. Stories in rhyme.] I. Adams, Lucas Grillis, ill. II. Title.
[E]-dc2 2003095189

Printed in Hong Kong

SCHOOL
Mable's Cafeteria
Mable's Ladle

Good morning, Mable with a ladle at the table.
Good morning, Jesse. What would you like to eat, mice or rice?
Please be nice and eat the rice, not the mice!

Silly Mable with a ladle at the table. I am a boy. Boys do not eat mice. Please be nice to the mice and give me rice, not the mice.
Good choice!
CEREAL

Good morning, Mable with a ladle at the table.
Good morning, Tyler. What would you like to eat, cake or snake?

Silly Mable with a ladle at the table. I am a boy. Boys do not eat snakes. Roadrunners eat snakes. The roadrunner can eat the snake but I want to eat the cake.

Good morning, Mable with a ladle at the table.
Good morning, Angel. What would you like to eat, legs or eggs?
Do not eat me! Help me get out.

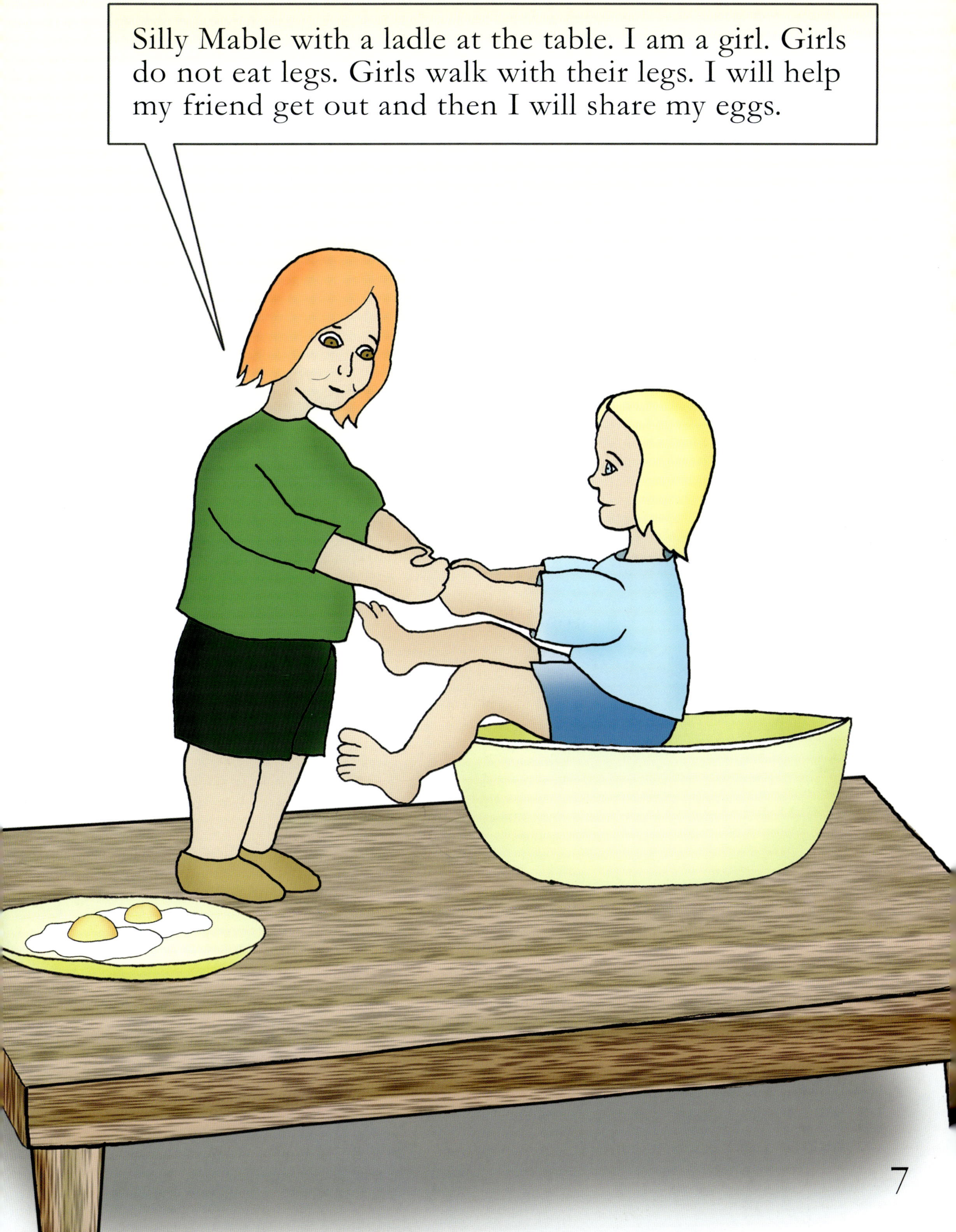
Silly Mable with a ladle at the table. I am a girl. Girls do not eat legs. Girls walk with their legs. I will help my friend get out and then I will share my eggs.

Good morning, Brandon.
What would you like to eat, peas or fleas?
Good morning, Mable with a ladle at the table.

YUCK! Silly Mable with a ladle at the table. I am a boy. Boys do not eat fleas. Boys eat peas. Give me peas, please.
What's worse? Being eaten by fleas or eating peas?

Good morning, Mable with a ladle at the table.
Good morning, Brianna.
Would you like to eat green beans or blue jeans?

Silly Mable with a ladle at the table. I am a girl. Girls do not eat blue jeans. Girls wear blue jeans. Please give me green beans.
I'll eat your blue jeans if you don't eat your beans.

Good morning, Joshua.
Would you like to eat a grape or a cape?
Good morning, Mable with a ladle at the table.
TAKE THE TAPE OFF MY MOUTH SO I CAN EAT MY GRAPES.

Silly Mable with a ladle at the table. I am a boy.
A boy does not eat a cape. A boy wears a cape.
If you give me a grape I can fly in my cape.

Good morning, Stephanie.
Would you like to eat a post or toast?
Good morning, Mable with a ladle at the table.
What about a ghost?

Silly Mable with a ladle at the table. I am a girl. Girls do not eat a post. Termites eat a post. I'll eat the toast and the ghost can eat a roast.
Best post I've ever eaten!

Good morning, Mable with a ladle at the table.
Good morning, Chow Fat. Would you like juice or a moose?

Silly Mable with a ladle at the table. I am a boy. Boys do not eat a moose. Boys drink juice. Give my juice to the moose and the goose, and I'll eat a chocolate mousse.

Good morning, Mable with a ladle at the table.
I dare you to eat the bear!
Good morning, Geoffery. Would you like to eat a pear or a bear?

Silly Mable with a ladle at the table. I am a boy. Boys do not eat bears. Boys eat pears. I will eat a pear.
See there, pear.

Good morning, Mable with a ladle at the table.
Good morning, Cassie. Would you like to eat corn or a horn?

Silly Mable with a ladle at the table. I am a girl. I blow a horn. I cannot eat a horn. I want to eat corn.

Good morning, Hopi.
Would you like to eat a hen or a pen?
Good morning, Mable with a ladle at the table.
I will get in trouble if I chew my pen.

That hen needs to go back in her pen.
Silly Mable with a ladle at the table. I am a girl. A girl does not eat a pen. A girl writes with a pen. I want to eat a hen.
HEN SCRATCHES

Good morning, Mable with a ladle at the table.
Good morning, Zed. What would you like to eat? Would you like to eat bread or a bed?

Silly Mable with a ladle at the table. I am a boy. Boys do not eat beds. Boys sleep on beds. I want to eat bread in bed.

Good morning, Amber. What would you like to eat? Would you like to eat cheese or keys?
Good morning, Mable with a ladle at the table.
We want cheese!

Silly Mable with a ladle at the table. I am a girl. Girls do not eat keys. Girls unlock the treasure chest with keys. Girls eat cheese, so give me cheese, please.
I am so proud of all of you for making the right choices!

PHONEMIC AWARENESS:

Definition: The ability to create new words by adding, deleting, shifting, and substituting speech sounds.

Levels:

1. Sound localization: Identifying the source of the sound.
2. Sound discrimination: Ability to tell the difference between two similar speech sounds in isolation; i.e., /b/ or /d/ or in words; i.e., "bean" or "dean".
3. Word awareness: Identifying the number of words in a sentence. There are six words in the sentence, "The dog is big and brown."
4. Syllable awareness: Identifying the number of syllables in a word. The word "mother" has two syllables. The word "popsicle" has three syllables.
5. Manipulation (add, delete, shift, and substitute) of sounds to create new words.

"Mat," take away /m/ (sound) = "at."
"Mat," add /s/ (sound) = "mats."
"Mats," shift the /t/ and /s/ (sounds) = "mast."
"Mat," substitute the /k/ (sound, letter "c") for /m/ (sound) = "cat."

The same changes can be applied to syllables: i.e., "depart" plus "ment" = "department."

PHONEMIC AWARENESS SKILLS TARGETED:

Substituting and deleting the initial sound. /r/ substituted for /m/ changes mice to rice. Leg minus the /l/ sound is the word egg.

SOUNDS TARGETED:

r/m, l/-, p/fl, b/j, k(c)/gr, p/t/g, m/g/j, b/p, h/k (c), h/p, b/br, k/ch

BASIC LANGUAGE SKILLS TARGETED:

Function; i.e., Ask the question:

"What do you do with food?" Response, "Eat food."
"What do you do with legs?" Response, "Walk with legs."
"What do you do with a pen?" Response, "Write with a pen."
"What do you do with a key?" Response, "Unlock (open) the door with a key."

Category: i.e., food.

Passive voice sentence; i.e., "Being eaten by fleas" (passive voice) vs. "eating peas" (present progressive).

Prepositions; i.e., on, with, at.

Conjunctions; i.e., and, or.

Pronoun; i.e., I.

Read the story each day for two weeks to be able to go through the entire sequence of exercises. In the beginning put pictures or other manipulatives on felt board and point to each as you say them. After they respond, count the pictures and congratulate the students for helping you. After doing this exercise a few times during the semester with different stories, discontinue using the pictures and manipulatives and try to get the students to come up with other methods of counting or remembering the words you say; i.e., use your fingers, clap your hands, etc.

***Phonemic awareness activities are complimented by whole language activities. Talk about the story with the students and ask comprehension questions; i.e., who, what is that, what is she or he doing, when, where, why.

Word Level:

Teacher: When you hear the name of a food pretend to eat and say "m-m-good."
(Say only one food and wait for response.)
Mice - Rice - Corn - Legs - Grapes - Bed - Cake - Snake - Ghost - Beans - Fleas - Jeans - Eggs - Cape - Horn - Peas - Bear - Cheese - Pear - Keys

Teacher: How many foods did I name?
Rice - Cake (2)
Toast - Pear - Bread (3)

Teacher: Say "rice - cake." (Teacher goes through above list using this example. You can also call this game "Hide the word." You can use the pictures in the beginning to help the students get the idea. Again, at some point discontinue using the pictures.)
Students: "Rice - cake."
Teacher: Now tell me what I forgot to say. "_____ - cake."
Students: "Rice."

Sound Level:

Teacher: Tell me if these words are same or different.
Rice – rice (same)
Cake – snake (different)

Sound and Word Level:

Teacher: Help me finish these sentences: (This can be done during the reading of the story after the children become familiar with the story. When the students have heard the story two or three times they can complete the sentences with the correct word when you pause.)

At breakfast I eat eggs. I walk with my (legs).
Do you want to eat mice or (rice)?
I sleep in a bed but I eat (bread).
Boys do not eat a snake. They eat a (cake).

Teacher: I am going to say a silly sentence and you help me by making it sound right. (After the children have heard the story several times you can vary this activity and do it during the reading of the story. Tell the students that they have to listen carefully because sometimes you read silly. Tell them if they can catch you every time you read it silly they will earn a special treat after reading time.)

I walk with my eggs. (I walk with my legs.)
I eat mice. (I eat rice.)
I sleep in bread. (I eat bread.)
Boys eat a snake. (Boys eat cake.)

Syllable level: Activities can be similar to above exercises but with parts of words instead of whole words.

Teacher: How many times does you chin move when you say these words? (Demonstrate by opening your mouth with exaggeration.)

Ma – ble (2)
Corn (1)
Hot dog (2)
Schoolhouse (2)
School bus (2)
Playground (2)
Beans (1)
Hamburger (3)

Teacher: Finish this word for me. (It is best to do this during the story after the students are familiar with the story.) Tell the students they are to listen and if you forget to say all of the word, they can correct you. For each correction they make you drop a token in a box and after the story count the tokens and reward them for good listening. Sometimes read the word with part missing; i.e.,

"Good morning, Ma____ at the Ta____ with a La____."

"Good morning, ___ble at the Table with a ____dle."

Teacher: Guess the word I will say. (In the beginning you can hold up two pictures. Say the words slowly with a break between syllables.)

Ma - ble
La - dle